THE BURDEN OF ALL THE BEAUTIFUL THINGS

THE BURDEN OF ALL THE BEAUTIFUL THINGS
by Andrew Buckner

The Burden of All the Beautiful Things Copyright © 2024 Andrew Buckner. Published by Requiem Press.

All rights reserved. No part of this publication may be reproduced or transmitted in any form or by any means, electronic or mechanical, including photocopy, recording, or any information storage and retrieval system, without permission in writing from the publisher.

https://requiempress.weebly.com/
https://awordofdreams.com/

Cover image Vecteezy.com

A Requiem Press Book

ISBN: 979-8-9899561-4-2

ACKNOWLEDGMENTS

As always, the following collection of verse is dedicated to my wife, Valerie, and my two daughters, Bianca and Arianna, whose love and support continues to keep the pen moving on the page.

Moreover, I would like to acknowledge that the poems "Third-Person Self-Portrait" and "Unboxed", which are featured in this collection, were previously published in the 55th edition of Roi Faineant Press, *I Can't Drive 55*.

On January 15th, 2024, Persimmon Lit published "The Mansion that Friday Built" and "Third-Person Self-Portrait" as part of their second issue, *Homestead*.

On March 31st, 2024, "I Refused to Believe in You. I Still Do." was published by Resurrection Mag as part of their Crucifixion issue.

Contents

A Puppet Can Only Move So Far In Either Direction **1**
The Burden Of All The Beautiful Things **4**
A Knee-Jerk Reaction To Sound **7**
The Words **8**
If I Listen Closely, I Can Hear The Ghosts **11**
After The Day's Long Servitude **13**
Unboxed **15**
The Blank Box Of Another Painful, Unspoken Christmas Custom **17**
A Moment To Heal **18**
Third-Person Self-Portrait **19**
The Mansion That Friday Built **21**
Now **23**
A Triumph Over Vanity **25**
And I Dream. And I Try. And I Dream. **27**
Fires Of My Own Making **28**
I Refused To Believe In You. I Still Do. **29**

A PUPPET CAN ONLY MOVE SO FAR IN EITHER DIRECTION

And the wheels are caked with dirt
And you can only feel
The push from the young child moving
The wheelbarrow
You sit hunched over in, back aching,
The "rush but be slow and enjoy it" nature
Of the muse—

A clump of hay where you step,
An indifferent attitude to the wall
Of art, modern day literary murals
You erect

And you breathe and look around
And see the mundanity of your features,
The scent of manure about your nostrils
And know that you are just another
Body going through the ever-accruing financial, mental
Stress of 21st century living

(And you will work and you will die
And you will work and you will die)

Just to end up broke,
Still beneath a landfill of earth,
Drowning without breath
Much like you did in life

And you tire of making sense of the direction
Others push you in
Just so they can say they control you
That they have their finger on your pulse
That you owe all your success to them

And you ponder that the rhythm is there
But, the passion, meaning behind it is lost
Like the subtlety, signposts of good storytelling,
In modern films, books, human mannerisms

And you ponder how many masters you look up to
That have lost their touch
Became a victim of the political obsession, paranoia,
That slowly gets the flesh of everyone
Beneath its fingernails via
The social media echo chamber

Kindness twists the air vindictively

And you end up ranting
Like all the other aging ghosts,
Flesh sagging beneath eye sockets
With a groan from the familiarity
Of the chains that haunt them

(And you will work and you will die
And you will work and you will die)

And everyone gets louder and says less
And the noise feels as if it is crushing, killing you
A jackhammer taken to tear down
And renovate a crumbling wall,
And the dining room they construct here
Is even more lonely, desolate, and alien

And your patience is gone, but you're
Supposed to carry on
And be a good little soldier
Even though you don't agree with the
War you've been thrown into
Because your choices are few

And a puppet can only move so far
In either direction

And you wait on a landing strip
Breaking rocks in a prison yard of
Your veins, organs, muscles, brain

And you wait for the warehouse shift to be over
With everyone around you laughing like your in a madhouse
While reiterating the same two subjects ad nauseam

And you wait and wait
On your wheels caked with dirt
For a glowing beam,
The extraterrestrial mother ship to come take you away

To find your own kind, meaning, purpose

To direct yourself on your own route

(And you will work and you will die
And you will work and you will die)

Again.

THE BURDEN OF ALL THE BEAUTIFUL THINGS

Sixth cranial nerve palsy,
A blurring of the eyes,
A doubling of the vision
Making items in the distance
Appear to simultaneously morph together
And pop-out like a 3-D image,
Particularly when overfatigued,
Particularly when night driving,
The result of overworking,
Overstressing,
Overtime,
Years of trying to provide
With fumbling but eager fingertips
For my family

Along with the playful belly pats,
Insipid allusions to the Pillsbury Doughboy,
Reminders of the late nights
I'd get home overworked,
Overstressed
From nearly six years of overtime
And the weight accrued
From eating quickly and going to bed
Just to repeat the anxiety-inducing cycle
Of unyielding warehouse labor,
The same etchings of the same motions
Over the tombstone of my days,
When morning arrives
Yawning, unwelcome, far too early,
Frankenhaired, pajama-clad,
And sleepy-eyed
Yet again

Call to mind the still-searing edges
Of the disturbing photograph—

The burned-in-my-brain
Images of aggression:
People crossing their eyes,
Imitating my ailment
In an infuriating mirror image
That was awarded an even more maddening
Bit of laughter from the jeering crowd
That gathers in my proximity
(And, among them,
Higher-ups, supposed "professionals"
Who weren't remotely acting
In such a manner
By letting such escapades escalate
To such a ghastly scene)

As if I can't see at all
The waters of insensitivity
That drown the human race
Or the lack of even a raft,
A saving grace
Splashing, hovering
'Round my stumbling,
Struggling extremities

As if I can't feel the
Sickening gut punch
From their words,
Punctuated again in childish,
Pantomiming gags,
Broken bits of jagged juvenalia,
About "carrying extra padding"
In direct response to my frame
From co-workers,
People who are supposed to carry
A trace of sensitivity, of thoughtfulness
Towards those around them:
Members of a so-called "family"

As if everything supposedly "different"
About me
Is a sheath of armor
That their dim swords of judgment,
Jealousy in its various forms,
Cannot penetrate

Thus, you cannot see the crimson bloom
Weeping from inside my shirt,
Hidden by my shoulders
And an expression,
A defense mechanism of indifference
Blocking their injustice

As if I cannot fully feel
The burden of all the beautiful things,
Like my introverted, woefully shy nature,
Like my ability to speak
Only when I feel comfortable doing so
And when I actually have something of merit to say,
Like the Tegretol I must take daily
Because of focal seizures that turned into
Full-on seizures nearly twenty-five years ago

As if I do not recognize
The misunderstood majesty,
The looming shadow
Of these perfect imperfections:
The tremendous traits,
The burden of all the beautiful things

    That makes me singular, unique.

A KNEE-JERK REACTION TO SOUND

Even the faintest pitches, whispers, voices
Call to mind a fork scraping across a plate,
My father, red faced, screaming
A list of all the ways I come short
Making even the most innocent bursts of laughter
Stirring from the twenty-somethings
At work, in my proximity, who are just trying to bring
A photo fast flash of holiday joy
To illuminate the socially mandated 12-hour shifts
The world gluttonously piles upon our backs like stones
With the promise of plentiful plates
And families with their own ecstasy woven
Into their laughter as days blend into
An indecipherable winter quilt the seamstress, I,
Must keep frantically twisting, knitting into
A perfect picture until sense is made
From the heat around my chest,
This knee-jerk reaction to sound,
A result of decades of unnecessarily saying
"I'm sorry"
And the core self-doubt which abounds.

THE WORDS

My words,
The pillars with which my soul ascends,
Were stuck, choking in my throat—
A cowering creature of darkness
With a tail shriveled towards the light
Whose muddled arms were pushed to the sides
Of my neck to stay lodged in place—
When called upon to read aloud in class.

(My heart still gallops,
A herd of horses stampeding in my chest, now
When the cinema screen of my mind
Replays such a horrifying scene
With the frantic stamina it did when
Such an event occurred several decades ago)

This creature, my social anxiety,
Possessed my core rigorously in my youth,
Especially in my high school years,
And he still looms as prevalently,
Features just as nightmarish, today
As he did when I was a kid.

Still, I'm trying desperately to keep
Him shackled, tethered, at bay.

The creature roars to life inside
When someone
Talks to me at work,
Which I usually reply to with a head lowered
To the ground, a quick response,
And the briefest look towards the speaker
And away in the best maneuver I can
Muster towards social courtesy.

I stammer and stutter when addressed
And a crowd of more than a few people
In a room makes the creature in me scream
Within, forcing my eyes to the nearest exit
As a tremor, the same panic in my heart
I felt when reading aloud decades ago
Abducts my sensibilities, digging its blade-like
Claws into the raw, pulpy flesh of my mind
And biting down upon it.

Yet, these words, beautiful beacons of eternity
With which I have been attempting to craft
A part of me that will endure long after my
Physical frame has withered, are never
Fully taken by the creature.
This is evident as I continue to reach
The horizon of my ambitions with them.

The anthologies of my short stories, novels,
Numerous full-length poetry collections,
And award-winning screenplays
I've crafted through these words, the ones which
Terrified me with the attention
And laughter they drew in adolescence
When spoken aloud,
Are now seen through the cloudy skyline of my
Lifelong ambitions, that of a writer, I now ascend.

The anthologies of my short stories, novels,
Numerous full-length poetry collections,
And award-winning screenplays have come
From my internal power struggle with the creature,
My social anxiety.
Though he wants to take credit for exposing
My weaknesses, filling my head with
Distorted views of how others see me

He is my greatest collaborator.

He is also my greatest foe,
The naysayer I dearly want to disprove.
Thus, I push myself to write.
Thus, I push myself to take baby steps
Towards being social.

I just want to look someone in the eyes
Without hearing your voice in my ear
When I'm addressed.

That will come once I reach the horizon.

I just want to offer a genuine smile
And enjoy the discourse that comes
So easily from my fingertips
But struggles to fly past my lips
With wings of volume, amplified magnificence.

That will come once I reach the horizon.

I just want the social confidence
Of the average individual.

I just want some appreciation from others
For the words that spill best from me
In silence.

That will come once I reach the horizon.

I see its palisades. I see its shadowy shape
In the distance.

I will reach the horizon
In due time.

IF I LISTEN CLOSELY, I CAN HEAR THE GHOSTS

If I listen closely, I can hear the ghosts
Of memories— kids scurrying, scattering, playing
Hide and Seek in the closets, corners
Of the quaint, two-story building,
Now as empty as the wine rack that
Was once the centerpiece of the kitchen,
As empty as the walls surrounding such sights,
That my mother has called "home"
For nearly two decades.

If I listen closely, I can hear my fiancé,
Now my wife of fifteen years,
Whispering how nice this new home is,
The Christmas bells announcing Santa's presence,
Presents wrapped, unwrapped,
Thanksgiving dinners made, eaten, recalled,
Seasons passing,
The sun rising, the snow falling,
The front porch, the backyard
Filled with drinks, napping adults, laughter, life.

If I listen closely, oh, cherished domicile,
I can hear your songs of comfort,
Sameness, oneness, change,
The lawn mower I pushed during the early
Summers of my mother's ownership of you
Roaring to life,
My long passed German Shepherd, Brandy,
Filling the halls with her warmth,
Clacking claws, excited barks, distinct verve.

If I listen closely, I can hear everyday objects,
Most of which are now left on the curb
Like foreign debris,

Tell their collective tales
Of experience, triumph, and woe.

If I listen closely, I can hear
Human shapes, forms move, grow
From children to adults,
Thoughts to realities
Multiplying in number, scale, and ambition.

If I listen closely, I can hear,
Oh, cherished domicile,
All that you know.

AFTER THE DAY'S LONG SERVITUDE

After the day's long servitude
Home welcomes me in red ribbons
And gold paper tidings—
Neatly constructed sheets of self,
A gift of solace among society's endless feuds

After the day's long servitude
Where I am eyed as a mere peasant,
Another twisted arm extending the corporate reach,
Though already infinite and limitless,
Home's extremities welcome my true features,
Thy kingly, poetic lineage with soft kisses, embraces
Daily whippings, wounds smoothed over
In the merry, reassuring songs she sings

After the day's long servitude
Where my body is not my own,
The zombie reiterates it's well-carved steps
And even fellow performers throw stones,
Home summons the taste of peppermint,
Spearmint, nourishment to the thirsting senses
And the contracting fingers of eucalyptus
To the aching flesh, the overused marrow

After the day's long servitude
Where the head feels bomb-like,
Repeatedly detonated in synchronicity
With each ticking second
And the acrid taste of bitterness, anger, bile,
Copper, blood tires of tap dancing on the tongue:
Home disrobes the too-taut garments of the Imposter
Syndrome sickening mankind;
A necklace choking free breath

After the day's long servitude
Forces both the fangs and the serpent
To unfurl from even the most benign entity:
Home quells the venom, massages scaly eyes
'Til cold crimson runs blue as waves
'Til the winter-like spring, summer, and fall
Of labor days casts our temporary hibernation,
'Til this gift of solace is accepted without hesitation

After the day's long servitude.

UNBOXED

As if returning a forgotten memory, like an abandoned child,
Back to the banks of the subconscious which violently pushed it,
Womb-like, away from my fleeting paternal grasp, my eternal awareness,
To live desolate, desperate, neglected, and alone in
What I imagine to be a plain brown box
In a chilly, musty, secluded basement, my mother,
In an act of shedding the echoing voices of recollection
Which embody the home I grew up in, the one from which she
Is beginning the process of post-retirement departure,
Casually hands me a palm-sized, black and white,
60-minute cassette tape
With the all-too-familiar, hieroglyphic-like penmanship
Of one of my fleeting friends from middle school on it,
A circle of sound that hasn't met my senses, hands
Since approximately the mid-90's
Along with a paper printout of my first full-length feature script,
Whispers in the Darkness,
Which I wrote with one of my best friends in middle school.

And as I note the immaculate condition of both items
And my finger traces over words, pages, wheels which once
Spun forwards and backwards in an endless cycle
In the now ancient, near-extinct beast
Us '90's kids once called "a tape player",
I can't help but think of how far I've come,
How little I've grown in taste,
How quickly friendships vanish yet stay the same,
And how art,
In all its various forms,
Is a time machine
Which, especially when stumbled upon without preparation,
Can connect you to a mindset, a person,
A younger, less experienced, but far more optimistic version of you,

As if attached with invisible wires which record your thoughts
In a taut, all white cat scan-like tunnel of claustrophobic screeches
And all-too-personal restrictions of movement and breath,
You're simultaneously happy to have unboxed,
Delighted to have grown into someone else from,
And yet, in the same instance, dearly wish
To avoid.

THE BLANK BOX OF ANOTHER PAINFUL, UNSPOKEN CHRISTMAS CUSTOM

"We can't afford Christmas this year,"
the voices of Christmases past
inwardly echo as if in sync with
your own gentle, understanding soprano
as it partakes
in what has become our own private
November/ December tradition.

And I, a halestorm of guilt brewing
in my gut as visions of how often I
put my writing over monetary
gain and
the pride I loudly exhibit over such
self-satisfying actions,
find myself directed towards
another seasonal rite:
this searing candle sense that I should've
worked harder, longer, and been more
focused on our financial needs and not
my own artistic ones;
another attack from the empty altar
society forces
all of us to eternally worship at.

And as red monetary thoughts, especially the
familiar ones that whisper sinisterly in my
ear that I should've been saving for this all
year and the silent vows they make me take to
do so next year, pad the now shortsighted walls
of my psyche
with a green that matches the mental vision I
have of the tree we have yet to buy as well as the
paper from various unbought presents

which will follow
in its wake, the blank
box of another quiet personal gut punch, another
painful, unspoken Christmas custom is checked.

A MOMENT TO HEAL

The world demands the chisel, the restless grunt
Of the laborer, warehouseman pushing, pulling,
Straining at the rusty, screeching, squeaking wheel
Of society's faux, idealized vision of success:

An unsympathetic beast
Bombarding the broken basement of doldrums
Who just
Wants the body to move, produce, replicate.

Yet, the true creative, rebel, body immersed in toil,
Sheens of sweat stabbing his aching, oily skin with
Beady blades, knows that revolution is the cinema
Screen embodying serene scenes of rest which

The spirit of the laborer, refusing to be crushed,
Turns to as sights of hammocks and feet dangling,
Late-night movies with endless tubs of popcorn,
A quiet moment while crafting a poem, a tale

Stirs the butterfly of contentment to drift upwards
From the milky cocoon of hourly pay, mechanical
Movements which bind him so the creature can
Touch the velvet skies of his own idealized

Visions of relaxation, success:

A book page gently turning, a library feeding
The wisdom of ages to the starving, sapling soul,
A footprint forever etched in the immaculate
Lawns of ambition, a fall leaf under the heel,

Family time, a moment to heal.

THIRD-PERSON SELF-PORTRAIT

A swarm of angry bees, a honeycomb of darkness,
Hovers behind the nerve-laden riverbanks of the swampy eye.

Spastic reverberations, seventeen years of breathless warehouse labor,
Shudders with an exploding anguish, a timebomb between the shoulder blades.

Thus, your back is arched. Thus, your heart is coffin, anvil heavy
From the barrage of emails, responses from publishers about your eagerly submitted writing,

You sigh every time you see because you know the pleasantly-worded outcome
Is rejection before your stinger-strewn, hive-like brain fools you with a burst of dopamine into

Clicking on the electronic retort: The orange construction cone placed in horizontal lines
Along the once promising roads of your lifelong passion. And you, again, sigh, swim in the

Upside down, marshy edges of your gaze as a sensation of drowning, a visage of your
Lifelong regrets, failures, childhood taunts that, like the yellowjacket, still cause a redness,

Swelling, itching beneath the flesh where your true self, naively rejuvenated with a youthful
Vigor to create a still-burning dream of setting the world on fire with your art, rises

Like a pimple that you can never quite get to, pop despite the lifelong scratching, indention

Of fingernails to wounded, infected flesh. And it is because your mind is so laser-like

In its focus on what is currently wrong that you can't see all you've done right.
You miss the happiness trickling down from your hard work onto the smiling faces

Of your children as they grow, learn, pursue their own pleasures and hone their own skills.
You miss the beauty of the fall leaves outside your home which reflect, like a mirror,

Your dedication to providing for your loving family. You miss seeing the progress
Made with your auteurship: The innumerable novels, short stories, plays, songs, scripts, and

Award-winning films that wouldn't exist if you didn't have the can-do spirit that hides in the
Closet of your marrow, sits on your shoulder, and whispers positive affirmations in your ear.

You miss the way the sunlight bends around your frame and admirably fills your form
When your back is bent, the tiny creatures are ready to attack, and doubt clouds the eye.

You miss the luminosity spilling from your fingertips, illuminating your every movement:
The quiet, kind-hearted essence of you being distinctly you.

THE MANSION THAT FRIDAY BUILT

Giddy laughter rises like the songbird
Over the painted white living room ceilings
Echoing a joy splashing multi-colored luminescence
With the endless loop of *Muppet* movies, jovial signposts
Of my own juvenalia that amplify with the frequent
Trips to the microwave to make homemade nachos,
Stale chips amassed with yellow shredded cheese,
To listen to the robotic ding of the green numbers,
The digital timer of the heater in sync with the punctuative explosion
Of kernels bursting, fulfilling their birthright, becoming popcorn
Which both of my daughters, then single digits in age,
Would entomb with hefty loads of salt,
A winter's snow, in a clear plastic bowl
So big we needed to use both arms to carry it.

Another guffaw, this one born of pure nostalgia,
Forms rings around my heart, throat
As I recall the feeling of familial community, love that has planted
Itself in the soil of my essence, an ageless imprint beneath the bark
Of my internal tree, as I think of the trips we made to the local gas
Station during these Fridays, my only day off during the five and a
Half years I worked at the plant an hour away from home, simply
To buy gummy bears or take advantage of the free coffee they would
Give away during the winter months to patrons.

From this bout of bliss, I ponder the endless cycle of dropping the kids off at and picking
Them up from school, the summer months when we would rush out to
The movie theaters on these Fridays of freedom
To see whatever family friendly fare
Was just coming out on that day, if only for the memories it would make
(And the large tubs of popcorn and blue Icees that would inevitably follow)

And the hysterics turn to tears of pride and joy as I realize this impenetrable
Foundation I helped build with the bricks of positivity, innocence, and happiness
Will build permanent homes for all of the souls involved, upbeat discussions that my children
Will whisper to their children and, quite possibly, their own children.

And the hysterics turn to tears of pride and joy as I realize that, despite the
Inevitable changes, deteriorations in the blueprint of our mutual recollection
That will occur, no amount of power, the forceful swinging of the mallet of
Cynicism or age, can tear down the majestic,
Chandelier-laden palace of these days:

The mansion that Friday built.

NOW

The familiar stuffiness of the emotive attic, heart,
Core with dusty treasures hid
Lifts, taunts the pajama-clad, curious children
Ever-creeping, hushing each other
During the midnight hour as they softly step
In an effort to not wake their parents, to sour
The silhouetted shadows: The mind
Which finds inferiority in every detail of my poetry,
Prose, and creative status. My kids
Ride bareback on a black and white Arabian mare,
Thoughts of my wife
Inviting me to drink blueberry wine with her
After the long wait of the work day is done

And all I can do is check the soul-sucking box, my phone,
Curse myself for missing the premiere of the new film by Scorsese
Yet, in the same breath, I realize that art
Is happening right before me

In the evening sky fading to gray,
The soft cricket-like sound heard in the distance,
The painful screech of the rickety porch swing
Upholding my frame,
The young goats with blue chains around their necks circling,
Running in and out of occupied stalls,
Horses snorting, pawing in impatient agitation at the ground
While teenage girls laugh and talk about Taylor Swift
Casually going about their equine grooming routine
In a relaxed, languid drift

And the sense of labor, community
Time simultaneously ticking and slowing down,
The recently tilled soil,
The dark yet innocent smell of hay,
Earth hanging around the nostrils,

The baggy sweatpants, crimson Ecko hoodie
That comes with the all-too-familiar October chill
Permeating the outward air, my internal bones

The "Where have you been all my life?" sensation
Of the attic door listening to you
And, in turn, revealing its own similar soul
Makes this familiar stuffiness addictive,
A rose blooming from an open hand
Which no longer holds the phone,
But exposes it with cracks askew,
Or the decades long obsession
With the art, the joy, the promise
Of what the future will hold

Because I realize,
In this instance,
The magnificence,
Splendor reverberating,
Already here
Outside of the theater aisles of my own vanity,
In every panoramic frame of the cinema
Of the now.

A TRIUMPH OVER VANITY

Suddenly, over decades,
The gnarled vine of my lifelong passions
Has withered, coiled with tail tucked, afraid
Of the snake-like impression I've fashioned

Through the smoke screen of memories,
The embarrassing charade
That has become my routine interests–
Glass surrounding a thorny palisade.

Suddenly, over decades,
The weight of intent is only perceived
In features too-taut, too-tired, too-familiar.
Thus, I breathe

Only to expel what has been pulling me down;
To rise with a mechanical crest
Formed from mechanical emotions, limbs; a crown
Of self formed from others, bruises, perceptions askew–

I jest–
Suddenly, over decades,
To just
Laugh, submit myself to a routine view

By telling myself such peaks are mountainous,
Though ultimately ruinous
To eyes that dare peer beyond the thin, torn curtain
Where nude sobs, visions of true self scream, too.

Though such mirth fills the labyrinthine soul
Fingers shrilly encircle darkness,
Lost in a void of artless control,
(Such is life! Such is life, I know!)

And the vampiric cycle of labor, bills, stress
(Such is life! Such is life, I know!)

Once more tells hands stinging with long-exhausted
Impulses to create, though a penny
Crying infant-like from the bottom of an ink black well,
That though my voice is unheard, but one of many,

Time will judge the burden of these words,
Buildings damaged by harsh winters of humanity,
Cold intentions carved now, though now unheard,
Will echo back in later years as thunder; fierce and free–

A triumph over vanity.

AND I DREAM. AND I TRY. AND I DREAM.

And it all feels artificial, like leather—
Sunken seats, breaths, in a crumbling theater
The rats with human faces scour
To find the emotions the world won't let you feel
So tightly in crushed ribs, loneliness,
Sticky floors, overturned popcorn buckets—
Hollow memories that were once joyous
Splashes upon the tongue
Back when I prided myself on eclectic tastes,
The artistic and the momentarily satisfying ones,
Before my mouth was zipped-up by age,
Repetition of thoughts, ideas, bold-faced lies—
The promise which has long cracked, dried my lips,
Temporarily wets my undernourished palate
With bits of food, creative sparks,
The world forces us to be grateful for,
To believe is a four-course meal.

FIRES OF MY OWN MAKING

Even the houseplants stare in indifference
At the sight of circumstances
Dusted, vacuumed, and vanquished to plumes
Of cleaner— the unaltered form of self,
Staring too at similar internal charades

As the fear of too much routine, too much change
Stomps his feet and smashes the potted garden of sentiments
While throwing fistfuls of dirt on the floor to get his way,
While pushing over the discarded basket, brain stem
And spilling gray thoughts, familiar pieces
Of holy laundry on the ground, next to the door
While setting it on fire, repeating the cycle,
And calling it "art", "life", "poetry".

I REFUSED TO BELIEVE IN YOU.
I STILL DO.

I swear I heard your voice, Heavenly Father,
Telling me in daydreams and in nightmares weeks beforehand
To take another route, switch to another lane
That fateful rain-soaked January
When time slowed to a crawl
And the front of my car became scattered metal
Gleaming in flashes of red and blue lights.

Yet, I refused to believe in you
And I still do.

I've glimpsed you, Heavenly Father,
And felt your presence
In a quiet movie theater, my personal cathedral
(As blasphemous as it may sound),
In moments of great art:
Pasolini's *The Gospel According to Saint Matthew*,
Scorsese's *The Last Temptation of Christ*,
The silent features of DeMille
As well as
The poetry of Shakespeare, Alighieri,
Ginsberg,
The songs of Tupac,
The worlds pulsating eternity
Through my own fingertips, writing,
The attempts to nail myself to my own cross
And preserve my bleeding body
For the masses
In vain.

Yet, I refused to believe in you.
I still do.

My childhood was filled with Sunday services, Heavenly Father,
Communion, giving and receiving Christ,
Hearing your holy word,
Singing songs of praise for you,
Drinking your blood,
And still your name rings hollow
Around the edges of my veins,
My heart, my soul—
A gossipy whisper in a church pew.

Because I refused to believe in you.
I still do.

END.

ABOUT THE AUTHOR

Andrew Buckner is a multi award-winning screenwriter and filmmaker.

A noted poet, actor, author, critic, and experimental musician, he runs and writes for the review site AWordofDreams.com.

The Burden of All the Beautiful Things

Andrew Buckner

The Burden of All the Beautiful Things

Andrew Buckner